M000284174

gifts of the rain puddle

"With all the grace and wisdom of writers and mindfulness teachers like Mark Nepo, Beth Kurland's *Gifts of the Rain Puddle* teaches and supports readers through the direct, experiential authenticity of her poetry. Her lens on human suffering as both a therapist and meditation practitioner makes this book not only a very useful guide to one's practice of meditation, but a primer on moment-to-moment relating to one's daily life. Poetry has that power, and in the hands of therapist and meditation teacher Beth Kurland, *Gifts of the Rain Puddle* goes beyond and behind words and into the light of awareness available in all moments."

—**Mitch R. Abblett, Ph.D.**, clinical psychologist.
Author of *The Heat of the Moment in Treatment,*
and *The Five Hurdles to Happiness(forthcoming)*

"Filled with heartfelt poetry, quotes and questions for reflection, this is a masterwork of practical wisdom, kindness and life's lessons learned. Beth Kurland shows how mindfulness, innocence, mother-nature, and inner knowing can shape our lives. She shares insights for healing and wellbeing. How to drop the unhelpful stories we tell ourselves. How not to look, but to really see! How a simple breath makes magic of an ordinary day, or serves as a lifeline from stormy seas to safe and sacred ground. How small daily steps lead to a life well lived."

—**Ken Nelson, Ph.D.**, Senior Director,
Kripalu Center for Yoga and Health, Stockbridge, MA

"If, as Beth Kurland indicates in the preface, writing is therapeutic, a medicine for the soul, then this book is a treasure for anyone who reads it and takes in its offerings. Interspersed with wise words of her years as a practicing psychologist, Dr. Kurland provides sage advice and succor for readers through her poetry that is instantly accessible and intelligent. This book is a positive step for improving the reader's outlook on life as well as upgrading daily living."

—**Zvi A. Sesling**, Author of *The Lynching of Leo Frank*
Editor, *Muddy River Poetry Review,*
Poet Laureate, Brookline, MA

"In *Gifts of the Rain Puddle,* Beth offers us the opportunity to notice. Utilizing her heartfelt reflections, she invites each of us to take the time to pay attention to life as it unfolds, looking not just at the large events which offer draw our attention, but also to seek out the little occurrences we so often miss. Awareness is an active process as we learn, through Beth's guidance, to take the time to apprehend the world, both allowing it to come to us in effortless awareness and in inactively seeking through noticing, looking, listening, feeling, touching, and tasting the world. Thank you Beth!"

—**Dr. Stuart Jacoby**, Ed.D. Clinical Psychologist

"Beth's book, *Gifts of the Rain Puddle,* is a good reminder that we are not alone in our thoughts and feelings. Her poems speak to the realities of being human and provide perspectives that are useful as we experience this thing called life. The guidance she offers helps us consider ourselves and others as we grow. This is one to have on your bookshelf!"

—**Melysa Friedman**, LICSW, clinical social worker

"Beth Kurland's insightful collection of poetry is a 'must read' for anyone seeking transformational personal growth, comfort, and emotional healing. On both a personal and professional level, Dr. Kurland's poems speak to the heart and soul of humanity."

—**Jessica Kahan**, M.A., Ed.S.

About the Author

Beth Kurland, Ph.D., is a licensed clinical psychologist, author and public speaker who has been in practice since 1994, working with people across the lifespan from preschoolers through adults. With a particular passion for and expertise in mindfulness and the mind-body connection, she specializes in using mind-body strategies to help people achieve whole-person health and wellness.

Beth is the author of the award-winning book *The Transformative Power of Ten Minutes: An Eight Week Guide to Reducing Stress and Cultivating Well-Being,* a Finalist in the Health and Wellness category by Next Generation Indie Book Awards. In this book, Beth offers a practical, step-by-step guide to help readers learn strategies that they can bring into the course of their day to transform stress and create greater well-being, with short, daily exercises that take ten minutes or less.

Beth has been writing poetry since childhood, and offers readers these poems, inspired from her own meditations, her work as a psychologist, and her life's journey to find presence, meaning and wholeness in each unfolding day.

For free audio and video meditations, and for more information about Beth and her writing, please visit her website at

BethKurland.com

WellBridge Books™ *is an imprint of Six Degrees Publishing Group*™
WellBridgeBooks.com

Made in the USA
San Bernardino, CA
04 May 2019

gifts

of the

rain

puddle

ALSO BY BETH KURLAND, PH.D.

The Transformative Power of Ten Minutes:
An Eight Week Guide to Reducing Stress
and Cultivating Well-Being

gifts

of the

rain

puddle

*poems, meditations,
and reflections
for the mindful soul*

BETH KURLAND, PH.D.

WELLBRIDGE BOOKS
An Imprint of SIX DEGREES PUBLISHING GROUP

GIFTS OF THE RAIN PUDDLE:
Poems, Meditations and Reflections for the Mindful Soul

copyright ©2017 by Beth Kurland

Published in the USA by WELLBRIDGE BOOKS™
An imprint of Six Degrees Publishing Group™
5331 S.W. Macadam Avenue, Suite 258
Portland, Oregon 97239 USA

ISBN: 978-1-942497-33-2

(eISBN: 978-1-942497-34-9)

Library of Congress Control Number:

2017956143

Cover Design: Eve Siegel; evesiegeldesign.com

Printed simultaneously in the United States of America, the United Kingdom and Australia

1   3   5   7   9   10   8   6   4   2

~ ⚜ ~

To the child in us all, who has never forgotten about the gifts of the rain puddle.

To Alan, Rachel, and Noah – For the gifts of love, joy and connection that have become the fabric of my life.

contents

Contents

preface

To my readers ~

I am a psychologist by profession, but a poet at heart. Ever since I discovered poetry at the age of six, I have been inspired to write. For me, writing poetry has always been a very private matter, something I did for myself, often scrawling my poems on scraps of paper and sticking them in a giant plastic bag where they lay dormant for decades. This writing has been therapeutic for me, a kind of medicine for my soul. It has helped me put words to my deepest feelings, given voice to my hidden yearnings, made sense of life's challenges, space for grief and sadness that I would otherwise push away, and offered a place to express gratitude for the joys in my life.

My writing has helped me get through times of intense grief and loss. It has inspired me when I needed courage, has given me perspective when I got caught up in mundane stressors, has provided me hope when I have felt most alone, and has helped me through major life transitions. It has been the safe space where whatever I felt could show up and be heard. In my adult years, as I have studied, practiced, and taught mindfulness meditation, I have come to realize that for me, writing poetry is a kind of mindfulness meditation in action.

My life's path guided me to my profession as a clinical psychologist. I first recognized my calling at the age of sixteen. It was something that I knew I wanted to do, the way you know your name or the town in which you live. I have found tremendous fulfillment in my profession, but it has also been an enormous privilege for me. I have had the opportunity to sit with people from all walks of life and all ages, and provide a sacred space for their stories, their deepest suffering, their personal growth. In their stories and lives, I hear the common humanity that connects us all, and within that connection, I realize, lies healing, in the recognition that we are not alone.

This short collection of poems, meditations, and reflections came about as a recent inspiration, as I felt called to share the healing power of poetry with others. As a psychologist, I sometimes read poems by other authors to my patients to convey powerful messages that might not otherwise be said so concisely, or with such impact. There is not always time in our busy lives to pick up and read a full book with an inspirational or helpful message. The advantage of a short piece of poetry is that sometimes, in just a minute or two, one's perspective can be totally transformed. It is my intention that these poems and poetic meditations will offer you that. I hope that within these words you will find some encouragement, validation, inspiration, insight, or a place for your own emotions to be felt and heard; I hope that these poems will allow you in some way to bring your attention to the present moment, and discover the power of being mindful, to this moment, and to the callings of your own heart.

A WORD ABOUT USING THIS BOOK

Beyond being a book of poetry, this book is also intended to spark contemplation and to be a journal for you. The blank spaces are an invitation for you to reflect and be present to whatever thoughts, feelings, drawings, musings, sketches, or doodles want to be expressed as you explore the offerings of this book. I hope that the poems, meditations, quotes and questions you find scattered throughout these pages will help you to discover the spirit and essence of who you are, and inspire you to be your best self. The blank space is for you to express yourself, to give voice to whatever arises in you as you make your way through this book. Give yourself permission to read with a pen or pencil or marker or crayon in hand and let the blank space be an opportunity for a kind of mindfulness meditation to occur, where you can let whatever arises be welcomed and have a home. Let each day be a new discovery for you, a new opportunity to give freedom to those parts of you that have been silent for far too long. Be playful and have fun. This is *your* journey.

PART ONE

awakening

the door

Welcome to this space.
Come, have a seat
on this couch where humanity sits,
these cushions
that hold the weight
of a thousand heart breaks.
Come bring your sadness
of the loss you cannot bear,
the anger that consumes you
like a fire gone wild.
Come bring your anxiety—
the one that keeps you awake at night
and acts like a barricade
between you and your life that awaits.

You are welcome here—
the part that holds deep shame
hidden even from your eyes,
the part that was wounded as a young child,
the dark thoughts,
the parts disowned,
unwanted,
unnamed.

There is no part of you
not welcome in these walls—
No part not honored

in this room of human suffering
and great strength.

For you are not alone—
You never were.
Did they tell you that?

You were never alone,
nor I.

In this quiet space,
this sanctuary of human emotion
come home,
come home
to the self that awaits.

~ ❀ ~

Today you might practice a variation of a loving-kindness meditation. There are different versions of this, so feel free to find the words that work for you. Notice what it feels like when you send this compassion to yourself and others.

Breathing in and out, first say to yourself several times: "May I be healthy and whole; may I be at peace; may I be protected and safe."

Then send this thought to those you care about, saying several times: "May you be healthy and whole; may you be at peace; may you be protected and safe" as you think of those you love.

Now send this thought out to the larger community or world—repeating it again several times.

growing pains

Funny how the sight of the deflated soccer ball in the woods,
the bat, lying on the icy ground
make my breath stop for a moment;
produce a pang in my chest,
my energy dropping
unexpectedly
as if I realized something
I had forgotten.

As if I remembered
that the little boy
who I used to chase and toss balls with
and dig with in the sand,
who used to fill our yard
with friends and Frisbee,
football games and treasure hunts,
and endless hours of soccer
has morphed into a young man
who is waiting to depart
on his next adventure.

Funny, I think
as if I'm surprised
that the seed I plant this fall
will grow into a beautiful flower
next spring.
Can we know something with such certainty

and still be surprised?
They said this would happen—
the people I smiled politely at
when they told me it all passes
"in the blink of an eye"
and "enjoy every minute."

I want to turn away
from the heaviness in my chest
but I turn toward it
and make room for the sadness.

I will stay here
just a bit longer at this window.
I have been here before.

I see not just the ball and the bat now
but the bare trees, decades old and more,
the boulders—immovable,
the sky, expansive—
the rose shrubs—naked, but waiting . . .
reminders
of this amazing cycle of life.

gifts of the rain puddle

I woke up from a funk today
of too many bills
too many emails to return,
not enough time—
From that irritability
that creeps in insidiously
like a dark shadow
ready to swallow us all
if we let it in.

I woke up to discover
that I inherited a small fortune!

Actually,
if truth be told,
would you believe that I forgot
that it was here all along?

My neighbor reminded me this morning—
the little guy in the overalls and dirt filled fingernails.
I saw him laughing hysterically
as he jumped in a giant puddle,
a leftover gift from the torrential rains;
as he soaked himself,
and went back for more,
then began running and shrieking
through the wet grass

with his unsteady gait
until he fell down in a heap,
all smiles.

I watched
as he became fascinated
by the blades of grass,
and even more animated
when he discovered the stones nearby
that he could grasp in his hands.

How funny
that you, and I, and my neighbor
can all look at the same sights,
the ordinary moments of our lives,
and see such different things.
It is a choice, what we focus on
after all,
is it not?

Perhaps waking up
is as simple as not losing sight
of the gifts of the rain puddle.

~ 🪷 ~

It's not what you look at that matters, it's what you see.
—Henry David Thoreau

Of all the thousands of things you might focus your attention on at any given moment—do you tend to focus more on the negative things in your day, or the positive things?

Do you catch the little "jewels" in your day?

Today, focus your attention on something that you might not otherwise have noticed or seen, something positive in your day. Keep your attention there for a minute or more. Notice what happens as you do this.

metamorphosis

Leaning against the window
curled up into a tight ball
like I've seen of yarn
wrapped around and around itself
she whispers to me of her secrets
that have torn at her heart
for decades—
hidden, even
from her own brave soul.

He tells me of things unspeakable,
unknown
even to the closest observer
who sees only
the Hollywood version of the actor,
giving voice to a story
that is so urgent,
so genuine in its telling
that it cannot go unheard.

They courageously venture
into unknown territory
as they explore the terrain and depth
of this common humanity we call emotion.

Sacred stories shared,
in whispers, and bellows

made of stone, and glass and straw.
In the space between the listening
and the hearing,
I watch in wonder,
as the strands of yarn unwrap
again and again
to reveal
at the core,
an authenticity
where true healing lives.

morning meditation

Awake
awakening
a new day arrives
my reliable companion, my breath
quiet, rhythmic
steady.

Waiting to see who enters
the space where the walls sit

who will come to visit?
what surprises?
what arises?
opening the door of my heart
to the invited and uninvited alike.

I watch with curiosity—
the itch
the clenching,
chest heavy—
mind fills with thoughts
busy, busy, buzzing flurry
just watching
waiting
as the thoughts fall away
and come again
revealing beneath—

the sadness tucked into the deepest corner,
the longing that has gone unnoticed ,
the stillness that holds it all.

I am grateful for this
cacophony of sounds
that awaken me,
that call me to attend
to the deepest parts of myself.

Feeling heard,
something in me relaxes
as I move forward
into the day that awaits.

~ ❀ ~

Take five minutes today, at the start of your day if possible, and sit quietly, meditate if you like, draw or write about anything that you would like to express, or go for a short walk outside.

How might taking these few moments at the beginning of your day shift how you go forward into the day?

unknown

You wonder why
I'm the girl with the red hat and black cape,
the one with the purple hair and piercings all down my ear,
you look at me and see what you want to see
the outcast,
the weirdo,
the one with the dark makeup around her eyes
and face hidden from view.
You think I don't know
who I really am.

Do any of us?

What you don't see,
what I don't wear on my body
visible to your automated eyes
is the pain
of every person
who has made assumptions
about me
without taking the time to get to know me,
Every person who has judged me
with their searing gaze,
their mean words,
their gestures
that have shut me out
again and again.

My sadness is no different than yours;
I bleed when I'm cut, and my tears are salty
like yours.

I am hurt,
but I am not damaged.
I wear my red hat by choice,
and my cape encircles me
in protection.

You may not know who I am,
you may not understand me,
but my resilience is as powerful as
any ignorance—
and from this place
will arise
a compassion
and strength
that even I can hardly fathom.

the vendor

Masks for sale,
personas, facades
come one, come all
take your pick
from the thousands that exist—
there is surely one for you.

Hide behind the frozen smile,
pose aside the brave soldier,
lose your voice to the puppeteer,
vanish amidst the laugh track
that comes again and again
through the still box.

They manufacture them, I see
from media and news,
movies and billboards,
bombarding us with images
of who we need to be,
what we need to own,
how we need to look.

Perhaps I'll go for the deluxe package,
the one that comes not only with a mask
but with a small trowel
to bury my soul
beside me.

~ ❀ ~

What masks do you wear, or have you worn in your lifetime?

How has the media or messages from others impacted who you think you "should" be?

How might you describe or envision your authentic self or "true nature?"

noteworthy

Can we measure our worth
as a cup of dry beans?
the length of that cloth?
the height of that timber?

Is it as concrete
as the change in my pocket,
as visible as the movie star
who waves to the recognition of thousands?

Or is it more subtle,
perhaps
like the seed that I planted in the pot on my porch
that glistens a sliver of yellow
and catches your eye on a sunny day;
or as simple as
the smile of her eyes
as she recognizes your loving face
and calls it home.

reminder

Now that I have woken
can I Awaken?

Will I go through the motions of my day
like a play, so rehearsed—
script so memorized
that I am half-asleep on stage?

Or will I make this day
pulse with aliveness
as if I have arrived on this planet
for just one day?

Reminder to myself:
It is a choice I make each moment.

~ ❀ ~

What does it mean for you to "awaken?"

Think of times in your life when you felt fully awake.

When you are most "awake," how are you living your life?

PART TWO

finding meaning

meditation to greet the day

Today
is the gift
of a new day.

What small treasures await me
if I choose to notice?
Might it be the greeting of the Japanese Maple branch
as it waves to me from the driveway,
or the eyes of a stranger
with her gentle glance;
perhaps the warm cup of tea
with its soothing aroma,
or my daughter's presence
as she studies in the adjacent room?

There is no other day
just like today.
How might I show up
with my best self?
What might I bring to this day?
What contribution awaits—
large or small?

Perhaps it is as simple
as being aware enough
to notice the paper dropped
from the pocket of the gentleman in front of me

and returning it to its owner,
or as uncomplicated yet profound as
giving my attention
without being lost in thought.

Today is a new day.
How I choose to meet this day,
as ordinary as it seems,
may make all the difference
between a life lived,
and a life lived well.

~ ✿ ~

Draw a picture or write words that reflect the self that you would most like to bring into your day today.

Connect with those parts of yourself and imagine how it feels to live from those qualities. See what kind of day you might create by doing this.

question

You ask what is simpler
than the juice from this orange
succulent, dripping
quenching my parched throat
on this scorching day.

And what is more complex
than this gift from nature
grown from the earth
in the southern sun
from a seed
smaller than my thumbnail
picked by the hands
of a man
who yearns of a life
he can only partially grasp.

sunset

Today I encountered the most serendipitous gift
as I was ambling along the road,
my favorite running route
passed the open field where the grass grows wild,
beyond the cemetery with the near ancient headstones,
just after the gravel path that leads to the pond.

Honoring fifty years on this earth
with the simplicity of this walk with you
I could not think of a better way
to celebrate this day.

And suddenly
it is as if tubes of scarlet, and deep peach and crimson paint
spill out over the horizon
lit on fire by the heat of the sun
creating a spectacle like candy to the eyes
that makes me stop in my tracks.

In a moment's time . . . it is gone;
fallen away
as the sun drops in the sky

but I am left with gratitude for this instant
reminding me
that the most precious of life's gifts
lie in these moments
that slip through our fingers but remain in our hearts.

~ ❀ ~

Enjoy the little things, for one day we may look back and realize those were the big things.

—Robert Brault

What are some little things within your day that you might tend to gloss over? (It may be as small as savoring that cup of tea in the morning, or lingering just a bit longer as you hug your partner or child good bye as you start your day.)

Enjoy one little thing today that you might not otherwise have remembered to enjoy.

immortality

Do I dare to question
the wisdom of this mountain
that has been in existence
long before I came to this earth
and will be here
long after I leave?

Do I question the strength
of this immovable piece of rock
carved out by some invisible artist
of the world
long before these roads,
this town
ever existed?

The mystery of this wonder
leaves me awe-struck;
reminds me
of my tiny place on this planet
and the refuge that is found
when I surrender to these majestic surroundings.

the stories we tell ourselves

The stories we tell ourselves
are dramatic
repetitive
exaggerated
silly
redundant
self-deprecating
frightful
sometimes delightful,
deluded
distorted
automatic
preoccupying.

The stories we tell ourselves
keep our minds engaged
in a routine chatter
that resists
the evolving of *this* moment.

The stories we tell ourselves
take up space,
take up time,
are often old news
packaged in a novel wrapping.

They are told in bold letters,
and a monotonous tone in our heads,
filled with an urgency that is deceptively important.

The stories we tell ourselves
come like unending newsfeed—

BUT what might happen
if we stop—
drop the story—
if we sit in the nakedness,
the bareness
of no story at all
and simply notice
what unfolds
in the space where the story falls away?

~ ❀ ~

Notice the "chatter" in your head today. What are the stories that you tell yourself as you go through your day?

Are these narratives helpful, unhelpful, accurate, distorted?

Notice the tendency we have to live in our heads, to be caught up in our thoughts—and see if what you say to yourself today might be nurturing, supportive and compassionate.

finding ease

That morning in Paris
just after dawn
head clouded with thoughts
I could not escape
pulling me toward darkness,
anger,
caught in a mind made trap
of negativity
focusing on everything
I could not control,
body tired from lack of sleep,
I put on my running shoes
down the stairs
passed a hotel of sleeping bodies
out onto cobblestone streets
in fresh, quiet air.

I start to run
passed unopened bakeries
and shops,
toward the Seine.
I mark the bridge in my mind,
my landmark
as I run
along path and water
passed early morning joggers,

passed anger,
passed November chill,
passed fear,
and judgment,
passed bridge after bridge,
passed my myopic world view
into open eyes
of understanding,
non-judgment,
this moment

passed the Eiffel Tower
running and running
breathing
each breath
a release
a reminder
feet keep running
passed blame
into self-responsibility
what **I** can change,
where I **choose** to focus.
It is a choice
and there is more than one view.

I run—
until my body tires of exhaustion
I run
until I unburden myself
of the heaviness that has weighed me down.

And in that moment
something shifts

as the sun rises
along the Seine—
as I take in
the Paris streets—
as I walk back
into my hotel
not knowing then,
how profoundly
everything has changed.

heart opening meditation

I awaken to this day
with an open heart.

Feet hitting the ground
I fully inhabit my body
and find my breath
as I allow my chest and abdomen
to fill with air
reminding me
I have the gift of this day.

How do I want to be in the world today?
What kindness can I bring?
How can I leave today
a bit better for having been here?

Each moment is a choice,
and today I choose
to embrace peace,
to see the good in the world,
and to recognize
that the only place where life can be truly lived
is right here, in this moment.

~ ❀ ~

As you grow older, you will discover that you have two hands, one for helping yourself, the other for helping others."

—Audrey Hepburn

What kindness might you show yourself today?

What kindness might you show another?

prayer for peace

In this sacred space
where time falls away
to reveal a memory
of a people, long gone
there remains a five thousand-year-old legacy
Very much alive—

I reach out to touch
this torah
that is a bridge
between three worlds.

My heart is full
with sadness and joy
as I strive
to keep alive
the meaning of this moment.

I pray for a continuity that has no end.
I pray for tomorrow.
I pray for peace.

meditation for inspiration

I find inspiration today
in this tiny seed,
the one that holds
a blueprint of an entire life
within its walls.

With water and nourishment
I know this seed will burst forth
into the whole of its being,
into the potential
of what it was meant to be.

And so it is for me.

I am unique,
like no other.
I have within me
the potential
to light up the world
even if only for a brief moment
just by being me.

How can I nurture myself today?
What kindness can I show myself?

If I take care of myself
body, mind, and soul
I will allow the most authentic parts of me

to show up today.
I will express myself
from a deep place of knowing
I will do
what I have come here to do.

~ ❀ ~

The whole secret of a successful life is to find out what is one's destiny to do, and then do it.

—Henry Ford

What gives you purpose and meaning in your life? It need not be anything grandiose. It could be as simple as bringing out the best in others as you interact throughout your day.

How can you nourish and nurture yourself to bring out the best in yourself?

How might you share your unique gifts with the world?

PART THREE

discovery

lost innocence

I think I'll forego the makeup today
and let my hair frizz
and put on sweats
and dance in the shower.

I'll wear the silly looking wide brim hat—
the one I bought on vacation in another lifetime
when the sun was so hot it burned my feet in the sand,
and you looked at me
and I felt like I'd finally come home
after all these years.

I'll go out in the rain without my umbrella
with these flip-flops
so I can feel the drips of water
sliding between my toes
and I'll shake myself off like a dog
when I get back inside
and laugh aloud.

I'll run around the yard playing hide and seek
and finding all of the good hiding spots
like the nook behind the shed
where no one would ever think to look.

And I'll paint the walls,
maybe just one wall,
with pictures of flowers

and sunshine
and falling leaves

and I won't care that it looks like a child's artwork
because I'm too busy
watching all of the colors blend together and change.

Then I'll build a tent
with as many blankets as I can get my hands on
and crawl under there with my flashlight and just wait

and wonder

what of life we miss

when we grow up.

~ ❀ ~

We don't stop playing because we grow old. We grow old because we stop playing.

—George Bernard Shaw

How might you bring more playfulness into your life?

What did you do when you were younger, but have since given up?

What might you do today to bring some playfulness into your day?

evening meditation

At the close of this day
as I prepare for the transition to sleep
I choose to let go of everything
I do not need to hold onto.
I let go of worry that is needless
and anger, that is hurtful,
to me or others.

I let go of tension from my body
as I invite in
with each breath
a deep relaxation
that will carry me to a place
of peace and surrender.

I trust
that in this evening's rest
my body will restore and recharge,
my mind will quiet,
I will rejuvenate for the day ahead
as I surround myself
in a divine blanket
of safety and protection.

I reflect on the joyful moments of today
and allow them to fill me with a warmth
that nurtures me
as I enter into
the twilight of rest
and surrender to
the darkness of the night that awaits.

~ 🪷 ~

Before you go to sleep this evening, focus on your breathing for a few minutes, and with each exhalation, invite your body to let go of anything that you do not need to hold onto.

Write down, or make note of anything that you would like to bring with you into the evening—perhaps moments of joy, feelings of gratitude, or a sense of peace or calmness in this moment.

last swim

It is the last swim of the summer
in this magnificent lake
that has become my favorite meditation spot.
The chill will soon bring other days
and I want to savor this one just one last time.

As I let the water envelop me
I am aware of a tranquility and stillness
unlike the waves I am accustomed to,
and in this stillness, and solitude of the season's end,
the tears begin.

I let my heart feel the grief
of this profound transition upon me
that has been coming to me in dead of night,
keeping me awake
as the past nineteen years
collapse into a single moment
that is hard to grasp.

In three days
my daughter will be on a plane
taking her three thousand miles to another continent
to start another lifetime,
a semester of adventure,
and I am left to ponder where all the years have gone
and whether I treasured each enough.

I breath through my tears
as my goggles fill with water
stopping to empty them,
and pausing to catch my breath
as the deeper sobs flood over me
like an unannounced wave.

It was only yesterday
that I walked on this beach
pregnant with excitement and expectation
as the possibility of all things
spanned endlessly before me
knowing "some day" would come
but feeling it another lifetime at least.

I am surprised how physical my sadness is,
these feelings in my body I have long forgotten.
The joy and gratitude and excitement have their place,
but in this moment
it is the sadness I make room for
and let wash over me
as I let go
of my role
of the control
of the illusion that I could protect her all these years
and let go into
trust
in the magnificent woman she has become
and trust
that she will be protected
in this uncertain world.

Suddenly I am swimming in a sea of tears
of all mothers
who have watched their children grow up
and begin their own lives —
and I am no longer alone.

No way to prepare for this,
yet it is upon me,
and I welcome it in.

Tomorrow will bring new dreams,
new possibilities.
Tomorrow there will be pride,
gratitude,
deepening connections,
but for now
I allow the water to enfold me,
cradle me,
I let the sun melt my tears
I connect to my breath
and let it anchor me
even as the waves of emotions
toss me wildly about.

perspective

Caught up in grumblings
of my day not going as I wanted
I was reminded
that happiness is a choice
of where we put our attention.

I learned this today
from the ten-year-old Syrian boy
I heard on NPR
who wants to become a doctor.

He said he chooses to be happy
because there is no sense not to be—
because there is nothing he can do
to bring back his arms
the ones that were blown off
in the war.

If this boy
is able to make such a courageous choice
in the face of such adversity
surely
happiness must be available
for us all to grasp.

walking meditation

Feet on the ground
one in front of the next
so simple to walk
so difficult to attend to each step.

Soles of my feet
connect me to this earth
such a distant concept
so easy to forget
that there is more than me and my immediate surroundings
and my life, and my day-to-day problems and joys
and my narrow vision.

this earth
which grows the food that I eat,
this earth
which houses seven billion people,
this earth
which holds the totality of time on its soil,
which has seen civilizations rise and fall,
which has known the greatest creations
and deepest tragedies,
which is filled with beauty much of which I will never see,
this earth which is our home.

Let me step forward
eyes open

sharing this space
with the whole of humanity
doing my part
to walk peacefully,
mindfully,
creating gentle footprints
that will leave their mark
long after I am gone.

~ ❁ ~

Imagine that you could leave footprints as you walk through your day today. Each footprint represents some way that you touched someone's heart, smiled at someone, helped someone, showed kindness, or contributed in some way to your own well-being, the well-being of others, or of the planet.

What footprints will you leave today?

mirror meditation

What if,
when you look in the mirror today,
you choose not to focus on your imperfections,
all of those things about your body
that make you feel
not enough.

What if, instead
you choose to see
beneath the wrinkles
behind the pimples
underneath the dark circles
beyond the scale,
to the self that is waiting to be seen—
the one that comforts your children in the wee hours of the night
the one that brings your creativity out into the world
the self that loves, and listens, and gives friendship,
the one that offers leadership, contributions,
that makes others smile when you enter the room.

What if you choose to see your body,
not as deficient, defective, less than—
but as the arms that have known a warm embrace,
the mouth that has spoken encouragement and wisdom,
the belly that has laughed from the joys of others,
the eyes that have filled with tears of empathy
and the legs that have traveled endless journeys.

What if you see the self that is pure compassion,
the one that is intelligent, artistic, loving, humorous.

What if, when you look in the mirror today,
what you see is the uniqueness, the indescribable splendor of you,
the magnificence of this person
who is like no other.

Maybe then,
you will know the essence of who you are,
and you will feel truly alive and whole
once again.

~ ✿ ~

Be yourself. Everyone else is already taken.
—Oscar Wilde

Look in the mirror today and find some quality or qualities that you genuinely appreciate about yourself.

Focus your attention on this for a few moments, and then call it to mind as you go through your day. If you have trouble coming up with something, call to mind something someone else loves or appreciates about you, and see if you might recognize this in yourself.

free fall

When I am quiet,
in the kind of stillness
that allows me to notice the flutter of wings at dusk
in the branch outside my window,
or the amethyst streak in the sky
that acts as a backdrop against the pine needles
as the sun falls,
I feel arise in me
a calling from my deepest spirit
to write
to create,
to share,
to bring to the world
what I am most passionate about.

Sometimes,
I would rather ignore this voice—
pretend that I don't see the changing landscape
as it unfolds over years, and decades
and half a century before me,
pulling me towards
an uncertainty,
an unknown
that excites, and yet challenges me at my core.

I'd like to stay in my quiet corner of the world
where everything is familiar

and comfortable, and easy;
where there is no fear,
no self-doubt,
no decisions to be made,
no one to approve or disapprove—
Where I can close my ears
to the passing of time,
and remain frozen in a life
that is still and all content.

It is almost dark now.
I can just barely make out
the dancing of the branches in the breeze,
and the silhouette of the giant oak.

The voice is louder though,
my heartbeat too,
as I recognize that I must trod an unfamiliar path
if I am to grow in this lifetime
if I am to be true to this unbounded energy within me.

Taking a breath
I think of all the others
who feared,
yet nonetheless leapt forward;
and it is my turn yet again.

Eyes open,
I step forward,
what feels like falling,
or walking naked in the streets—
taking with me my emotions,
trusting
that my parachute
will catch me from my free fall.

~ ❀ ~

*Twenty years from now, you will be more disappointed
by the things that you didn't do than by the ones you did
do. So throw off the bowlines. Sail away from the safe
harbor. Catch the trade winds in your sails. Explore.
Dream. Discover.*

—Mark Twain

What does your heart desire to do that you have not taken steps
toward because fear gets in the way?

How might you take a small step out of your comfort zone today
toward something that is meaningful for you?

invisible ties

While I sleep,
you are waking on the other side of the world
as you buy a pastry and hurry to class.

While I sleep,
children are bathing in hand filled make-shift tubs
in a tiny village with no running water,
and playing soccer with a ball made from paper.

While I sleep,
a new day is beginning
and there are people watching a magnificent sunrise
as they greet the day.

While I sleep,
wars are being fought,
young men and women are risking their lives
and parents are grieving.

While I sleep,
children are dancing in the moonlight,
cities are bursting with activity
and someone is discovering the next scientific breakthrough.

While I sleep,
lives are being made in a warm embrace
and crops are being picked
that will end up on my dinner table in several weeks.

While I sleep,
the whole of humanity
is breathing
on this planet,
as we share a connection
that is impalpable—
so easily forgotten—
yet is as real
as the words on this paper,
that remind me
of the interconnectedness
of all things.

message to myself

In this life,
you will be given amazing blessings
that will become so commonplace
that you will begin to hardly notice them
for the treasures they are.
Do not take them for granted—
for everything is transient.
Bring gratitude with you, as you see with your heart
and discover the joy in the ordinary moments
of each passing day.

In this day,
you will be prone to get trapped in the busyness of the hour—
the list of things that must be done
in order to attain some illusionary sense of accomplishment.
Know that true peace
comes not in completing your to-do list
but in taking the time to pause,
to savor,
to appreciate,
to connect—with yourself and others—
and to replenish
so that you go through your day
with a sense of balance,
a feeling of being centered
and an ease that allows you to handle the unexpected challenges

that come your way.

In this hour,
you will be tempted to push away your feelings
especially the difficult ones—
the sadness, the loss, the fear,
but in doing so you push away with it the whole of who you are.
Turn toward, not away—
embrace these parts of you and hold a space for them,
for in them lies the depth of your being
your healing, and your growth—
the capacity to experience the fullness of life.

Make the ordinary sacred,
create time to be,
accept whatever you are experiencing within—
and trust that you have everything you need
right here,
in this moment.

~ ❀ ~

Take some time to reflect on and write down a message that you would like to communicate with yourself, from the wise, knowing part of you.

Think about what is most important to you, what insights you have learned, and what you would most like to remember about living your life fully.

PART FOUR

growth

invitation

When stress sneaks in
like an unwelcome guest
and puts up rigid walls
that I cannot see past,
it is the invitation
in a piece of pink, speckled sky
that calls out to me,
reminds me,
to slow down
to the rhythm of my breath
and open up my heart.

~ ❁ ~

Let stress be your friend today. As soon as you notice that stress arises, use this as an opportunity, a cue to become mindful. Pay attention to how you are feeling. Stop and feel this in your body.

Ask yourself what it is that would be most helpful right now. Perhaps it might be as simple as sending yourself some compassion.

morning rains

I'm grateful for the rain today
the steadfast kind that sounds like
ethereal travelers on my roof
and soaks the earth like a dry sponge.

I am grateful for this opportunity to pause
instead of heading out for my usual run in a timely manner;
this opportunity
to linger just a bit longer,
these extra moments
to discover the depth of emotion
that has been waiting for my attention.

In the past,
I might have felt frustration
for this wet day and hampered plans,
but today I welcome it
and see that in the space between the doing
is the invitation to attend to the most authentic parts of me
that wait so patiently to be revealed.

finding center

When I find myself spiraling out of orbit,
being hurled through the space of intensity
that feels overwhelming,
facing emotions that seem, in the moment
too difficult to bear,
I like to imagine that my feelings
are like giant ocean waves
cresting and crashing near the shore
and I am watching
from solid ground,
sand beneath my feet
connected to the stillness of the earth.

Each breath,
another wave of emotion,
some stronger, some smaller,
each calling to sweep me away.

But for the safety of this vantage point
I would surely be pulled into the undertow.
Yet somehow I remain grounded,
witnessing this dance of breath and wave,
observing
the power
of the human heart.

~ ❀ ~

What grounds or centers you?

When you are caught in the intensity of emotions, what most helps you find that place of calm within, like the eye in the storm?

How might you practice inhabiting that place of center for short moments throughout your day?

through fresh eyes

Sometimes I see with my eyes closed.

Do you?

I drive on the same roads
and end up at the same location
without noticing what I passed
or how I got there.

Sometimes I listen without my ears.
I am so caught up
in the thoughts in my head,
in the script I have rehearsed,
that I miss the unfolding conversation
with those I most cherish.

But other times,
more times,
I see with my eyes open.
Like today–
on my usual loop around the pond
the loop I have travelled a hundred times,
I noticed the house in the far distance
that looked like it was floating on water,
and the little girl with her dad,
watching her brother riding his bike for the first time.
And I felt a pull in my chest

as I remembered another lifetime entirely
or two
it seems
where I was both parent, and child.

I saw the gesture,
the invitation
to listen to the part of you
that wanted to be heard,
and I saw past the unfinished chores
to the part of myself
that just wanted space to be
without having to accomplish
anything at all.

We have these glorious senses
that connect us with everything important—
the feel of the sunshine as I walk to my car,
the sound of your laughter,
the taste of this food,
the colors of the sky—
and yet it is as if
they fall into slumber
during our waking hours.

I will make it a point
to wake up today.
I see the reflection of the tree branches
on my computer screen as I type these words
reminding me
that everything can be looked at
through fresh eyes.

~ ❀ ~

Life is not measured by the number of breaths we take,
but by the moments that take our breath away.

—Maya Angelou

What are some moments in your life that have taken your breath away?

How about in this past week, or today?

nightfall

Sitting near the edge of the woods
at nightfall
alone, but far from lonely
I am reminded of the peace that comes
with such stillness.

The branches seem to wave to me
as they dance skyward
in the moon's reflection,
and the crickets sing with the breeze,
making me feel quite welcome
in the near dark.

Funny how I can see more clearly now,
how my life is a series of moments–
points in some construction called "time"
where what truly matters
is what I am present to wholeheartedly.
It isn't the achievement or accomplishment
but the feel of the earth beneath my bare feet,
the way my daughter's voice sounds
when she is excited
and the intangible grief held
between myself and the patient in my office.
It is the quickening of my pulse
when I feel enthusiasm,
and the space where my anxiety rests

when I hold it tenderly.
It is the laughter of loved ones
and the longing of my own heart
when I stop long enough to listen.

As blackness descends,
the light of the stars
remind me of what is revealed
when time, and I, stand still.

Straddling between two worlds,
the lifetime I have journeyed,
and the one yet to be,
I surrender to the uncertainty
and embrace the wholeness of this moment
that connects me to life itself.

~ 🪷 ~

The future depends on what we do in the present.
—Mahatma Ghandi

What gestures and actions might you choose today that will have ripples well into the future?

false spring

Funny how the warmth of this winter day
lures me into thinking that spring has arrived and that the footsteps
of the passengers on this trail,
(etched in mud like the handprints my daughter
used to make at preschool before she grew into a young woman),
will not be covered yet again by another snowfall.

What kind of deception of nature is this, that plays with our emotions
and makes us think that what we see is so,
when, in fact, it is as temporary as these moods
which tumble like a stack of blocks
piled too high,
only to be built again by the eager hands that created it.

Nothing is enduring, though we grasp as if it is–
as if in the grasping we can hold the bits of sunlight
that slip through our fingers
on this warm February day,
as if in the clinging we can capture that magnificent wave
before it crests and dives
and becomes one with the sand and ocean all at once;
as if
in the holding on
I can keep you alive until eternity.

I marvel at the bare woods
that is the home to so many living inhabitants

and I bask in the warmth of this hour
as I let my skin be caressed by this passing gift.
Perhaps it is that knowing
that allows me to transcend time and space
for just a moment,
to value this day all the more
and to lose myself
in the scent of the pines
and the feel of dirt
and rock beneath my feet.

ordinary day

It's just an ordinary day
the kind that you might find on a postcard that they sell
at the gift shop off the side of the highway
mixed in with the cheap plastic jewelry
and key chains and peanuts—

the kind of day that comes often and feels routine
where you wash the dishes and throw in a load of laundry and
hustle the kids off to school and show up at work having wished
you could have savored that cup of coffee just a bit longer;

or the day where you do your life so automatically that it is like a
dance that you have memorized with such certainty that you can
execute the moves with your eyes closed—

but there is nothing ordinary about the volumes of blood your
heart is pushing through you to nourish every cell,
or the roots that push forth a sprout that will break through the
top of this soil like a rocket ship blasting through space,
nothing ordinary about our earth
being held in its gravitational force,
that same force that keeps me from floating away as I write this,
nothing ordinary about the way his smile creates a feeling of
safety and allows the viewer to relax
and feel a loving, warm feeling in her heart.

There is no ordinary day
nor hour, nor minute

and the enormity of that realization
hits me
as I sit across from you
sipping on my tea
listening to you sharing your passions,
then take the check, pay the bill,
and walk back to my car
sensing that something important
has shifted.

~ ❀ ~

How might you take an ordinary moment in your day and turn it into something extraordinary?

(For example, in a conversation with someone today, you might truly look into their eyes, attend to them, and give them your full presence. Or perhaps you might savor a meal slowly and delightfully.)

door number three

What if, behind door number one
I get to control every aspect of my life,
I get to leave all angst of "not having control" behind me
but the catch is that I must control everything—
including the behaviors and choices of those around me.
No anxiety or worry behind this door.
Is that the life I would choose?

And behind door number two
I could remove all uncertainty in my life,
by knowing exactly what was going to happen,
and when.
No angst of unpredictability in the lifetime behind this door.

And behind door number three,
well . . . there is uncertainty,
there is the unknown . . .
I can control only <u>my</u> own behaviors and reactions,
and I don't know how life will unfold
moment to moment.

I think I'll take my worry with me on this journey,
the not knowing,
the uncertainty . . .

For in all its difficulties being human in this life,
the alternatives

are far less appealing
than at first they might seem–
and what I wish for is not really control
or certainty after all,
but the trust and faith and strength
to go forward with an open heart.

proposal

As if the bench could speak
it calls to me to come sit
for just awhile,
to settle into this space
which is so peaceful, serene,
so that I can savor it just a bit more—

to pause and watch the ducks,
mother, and babies in tow,
as they scurry into the water
to the vibration of my passing footsteps,

to stare in wonder at the twinkling of the sunlight hitting the water
that looks like fireflies sparkling in the night sky;
to let the mix of breeze and warmth of sun
blend together like a delectable concoction of the senses,
to the tune of the geese singing a cappella in the background.

I feel so at home in nature's playground
like a child who has forgotten how fun it is to let her spirit run free,
but I am called by responsibilities that await
and I must defer your invitation
for another day,

knowing that for now
this momentary stroll
has been enough
to replenish my soul.

~ 🪷 ~

What do you do that replenishes your soul?

What allows you to "reset" from the busyness or challenges of your life?

How might you incorporate this opportunity to replenish and reset more into your day and week?

PART FIVE

coming home

just one breath

When sadness appears
or grief tugs at my heart
or anger threatens to kidnap me
or fear begins to swallow me up,

it is my breath,
just this one breath,
in this moment
that arrives like a lifeline
to carry me to safe ground.

the power of a few minutes
—a meditation

Breathing in,
I draw in serenity,
strength,
peace,
vibrant energy—

Breathing out,
I release stress,
angst,
worry,
tension,
and all that I do not need.

Breathing in,
I help my body restore,
recharge,
filling myself back up
to share good in the world
through my very presence.

Breathing out,
I choose to let go
of what is not serving me—
my negativity,

irritation,
need to rush
and self-imposed pressure.

As my breath slows,
so too do I
as I open to gratitude,
to perspective,
to the big picture of what is most important today.

As my breath deepens,
so too does my understanding
that in this moment
is everything—
that within me
are all the resources
to go forward with compassion and openness.

Pausing for yet another round of breath,
I feel the rhythm
of the life force within,
I feel the waves of emotion
pulsing through me
unhindered—

and I know
that I am better
for having taken this pause—
just a mere few minutes of clock time,
barely a blip in my day
and yet somehow,
something profound has occurred just the same.

~ ❀ ~

Find a few minutes within the day when you can take a pause. Notice what shows up in this space between the doing and the busyness.

Use this empty space to draw or write or express whatever wants to show up.

home

Awaken ye sleeper
ye seeker
you, with the sad heart,
you rushers
you hiders—
come you, with the story to tell,
the one who wants to be seen
and the one who never does.
Come from childhood and old age,
come from wisdom and naivety,
come if you know the answer
or if you know there is nothing to be revealed at all.

Come, sit in the circle
where hearts mend and share and cry and grieve,
where care is plenty
and sorrow is welcome,
where you do not need to be fixed
but simply heard,
where you do not need to push anything away
because there is space enough
for your deepest fears
and your greatest dreams.

Come, leave your shadow behind
the one that you have been carrying far too long,
come you, who have been looking for that illusive happiness

in some future corner of your mind
never quite able to be discovered.

Come into this moment
that awaits,
this moment
that connects us with invisible threads,
that remind us of our shared humanity,
that cradles us
in this precarious, glorious space
where we feel most alive.

Come, you are safe here—
no one to impress
no one to prove your worth to
nothing to achieve—
for you are accepted just as you are
and all parts of you are valued.

Awaken
to all of experience
to the highs and lows
the ebbs and flows
of this life

There is no goal, no finish line to get to.
You have arrived.
Settle in,
for there is no place else to be.

~ ✿ ~

Think of or imagine what it feels like to be "home"—to be in a safe space where you can be fully yourself. When in your life do you feel "home," and with whom?

See if you can call up a feeling of being "home" right now and let your body rest in the warmth, safety and acceptance of that feeling.

unexpected daffodil

The daffodils
in our front yard
are a gift from the previous owners,
how wondrous that they come up
year after year
to signal the first signs of spring,
as if to wake me out of my winter hibernation
and remind me of the changing seasons
and passage of months, and years
and lifetimes it seems;

funny that I almost forget each year
that they will arrive;
like surprise visitors
ready to share their cheerful essence
for but a passing moment.

But the daffodil in the woods
that I spotted this morning on a walk down the street
was a true unanticipated discovery,
hidden from view through my car window,
and almost tucked beyond the curve of the road,
thanks only to my unhurried pace
that allowed me to notice it there.

Blown from the seeds of its more intentional neighbors,
so unassuming in the woods amid the near barren trees—
a reminder
of the jewels waiting to be uncovered
when we take the time to observe
what is in front of us after all.

facing fear

Today I sat with my fear.
Frankly, I would have rather
checked my emails,
or folded laundry,
or gone for a run.
I coaxed myself
to sit in the room with It—
heart racing
and worry thoughts cascading
and all—

And something interesting happened.
I was able to see
all of those old, vulnerable parts of me,
all of those places from my past
spilling over into one giant heap
of fear.

And all I could do
was send some compassion to myself—
bring myself back to <u>this</u> moment
over and over
even as my mind wrestled with me to reside
in past and future—
Feel my feet on the ground
and know that in time,
this too would pass.

~ ❀ ~

When you reach the end of your rope,
tie a knot and hang on.
                    —Abraham Lincoln

What does courage feel like to you?

When have you felt it most vividly?

How might you access the courage that is within you, to help you face some of the challenges in your life?

sitting with unease

How much easier
to get up and go—
to throw myself into
my to-do list
than to sit on a couch
and breathe.

Because the sitting means
being with the discomfort
that gnaws at my core.
It means breaking out of
my automatic
comfortable mode
of staying busy.

In the sitting
I notice the unease in my body
like a cord wrapped tightly,
a constriction
with protective walls.

Turning toward these sensations
something in me relaxes
like being listened to
by a dear friend.

And in that space
I see the illusion of my thoughts
that would have me believe in their Truth.
I see the passing nature
of the sensations
as they come and then go.

In the sitting
I picture myself in a lazy river
flowing with the current
instead of resisting it
as I am so inclined to do.

And suddenly I am aware
not just of my own breathing
but of the rain as it falls,
soaking into the desperately dry earth
and of the plane overhead
carrying someone home
after a long journey.

When I open my eyes
I feel more space inside of me—
as if there can be such a thing—
and I sense that I too
have soaked in some nourishment
from this passing storm.

wake up call

It wasn't a loud thunk on the head
or a mystical experience
or a hit rock bottom awakening

it was the subtle feeling in my chest,
a deep, vague ache
of a moment lost,
never to be recaptured—
that reminded me
how sometimes the things that are most important
can slip through our fingers
if we don't pay attention.

~ ❀ ~

Today, ask yourself: When I look back on my life, how do I most want to be remembered?

How can I show up today like that person?
(For example, if I want to be remembered as kind, how can I show someone kindness today? If I want to be known for having an adventurous spirit, how can I live that way today?)

dichotomy

If I am honest with myself—
which is sometimes easier not to be—
I must admit the sadness knocking at the door,
wanting my attention.

It is big and deep
Lifetimes ago
and right HERE
reminding me that things are always changing,
that there is a letting go
even as there is a letting in.

Sometimes I grasp for my old life
to fill the quietness of this big house
of our "empty nest"
that is oh so full.

And therein lies the dichotomy
of this life.

My sadness is so physical
I can almost touch it—
in my chest, in my heart.
Easier to turn away
pretend it's not there—
but I hold it tenderly nonetheless.

And at the same time
is a vibrancy, an energy, an aliveness
of something new growing around me
that keeps me abuzz with excitement
in the wee hours of the night.

It is not an either/or—
I don't get to choose one and not the other.

So I let them sit side by side—
space enough for all three of us

lifetime companions on this ever-evolving journey.

longing

The drums on my roof
play a familiar song
to the tune of the falling rain
that nurtures the earth.

I haven't found the sun for days
and was beginning to fret—
but for the joyous rush of the waterfall
on the path in the woods
that has not flowed for a year.

And so I remind myself
on these gray and rainy days
of what growth awaits
when we can be patient
and listen to the rhythms on the roof.

~ ❀ ~

In the middle of every difficulty lies opportunity.
—Albert Einstein

In what ways have you turned difficulties or disappointments into opportunities?

How have you experienced resiliency in the face of challenges?

wish for you

Dance around the living room dear
the way you did without a care
when there was no audience to please
and you could listen
to the longings of your heart.

Draw a silly picture dear
no need to make it pretty or pleasing
just let it flow
the way you did before there were judging eyes
and grades
and right and wrong.

Take this pen, and write that unspoken story
and sing at the top of your lungs
because you have a song to share
and it doesn't matter
how many likes, or clicks, or views you get.

This one is just for you
and you alone—
put down your phone
turn off the screens
don't check your mail—

you have a dance, a song, a story
that is longing to be expressed

in this fast-paced world
where so much is suppressed
there is still time
to find your voice

it is a choice
whose choosing
is the difference
between status quo
and all that matters most.

~ ❀ ~

*People say that what we're all seeking is a meaning for
life. I don't think that's what we're really seeking. I think
that what we're seeking is an experience of being alive,
so that our life experiences on the purely physical plane
will have resonances with our own innermost being and
reality, so that we actually feel the rapture of being alive.*

—Joseph Campbell, *The Power of Myth*

What is it that makes you feel most alive?

What time in your life did you feel most alive? What did you learn
about yourself then that might be helpful for you now, to help you
bring that feeling of aliveness into your life?

What could you do in your life today, and on a regular basis, that
would bring you some small feeling of aliveness?